GALE
CENGAGE Learning

Novels for Students, Volume 16

Project Editor: David Galens

Editorial: Anne Marie Hacht, Sara Constantakis, Ira Mark Milne, Pam Revitzer, Kathy Sauer, Timothy J. Sisler, Jennifer Smith, Daniel Toronto, Carol Ullmann Research: Sarah Genik

Permissions: Debra Freitas, Shalice Shah-Caldwell

Manufacturing: Stacy Melson

Imaging and Multimedia: Lezlie Light, Kelly A. Quin, Luke Rademacher Product Design: Pamela A. E. Galbreath, Michael Logusz © 2002 by Gale. Gale is an imprint of The Gale group, Inc., a division of Cengage Learning Inc.

For more information, contact
The Gale Group, Inc.
27500 Drake Rd.

Farmington Hills, MI 48331-3535

Or you can visit our Internet site at
http://www.gale.com

For permission to use material from this product, submit your request via Web at http://www.gale-edit.com/permissions, or you may download our Permissions Request form and submit your request by fax or mail to: *Permissions Department*
The Gale Group, Inc.
27500 Drake Rd.
Farmington Hills, MI 48331-3535
Permissions Hotline:
248-699-8006 or 800-877-4253, ext. 8006

of the editors or publisher. Errors brought to the attention of the publisher and verified to the satisfaction of the publisher will be corrected in future editions.

ISBN 0-7876-4899-X
ISSN 1094-3552

Printed in the United States of America
10 9 8 7 6 5 4 3 2 1

Fathers and Sons

Ivan Turgenev 1862

Introduction

Ivan Turgenev's *Fathers and Sons* was originally published in 1862 in the Russian magazine, *Russkii vestnik (The Russian Herald)*, under the title, *Ottsy i deti*, and is also known as *Fathers and Children* in some translations. Even before its publication, the novel ignited controversy. The generation gap between the fathers and sons in the story neatly symbolized the current political debates between the older reactionaries and the younger radicals. The character of Bazarov, a young radical who declares himself a "nihilist," somebody who accepts nothingness, particularly inflamed both sides. Although Turgenev claimed at one point that he meant the book to be a favorable depiction of the young radicals, this group viewed Bazarov as a spiteful caricature of them. Many of the older liberals did not understand the book and were also very upset at the influence that it had on the young radicals, who claimed the term "nihilist" for themselves, and used it in their violent protests.

Despite the initially scathing reviews, the book has stood the test of time, and many regard it as Turgenev's best. The book also represents the times, depicting the social unrest that was present in Russia just prior to the historic 1861 emancipation of the serfs—Russian slaves that were owned by the landed nobility—by Alexander II, as well as the various reforms that were in place at the time.

Author Biography

Turgenev was born on October 28, 1818, in Orel, a provincial town in Russia. His mother, Varvara Petrovna, had inherited a large amount of land, and the estate of Spasskoe-Lutovinovo was the largest and most impressive of her holdings. It was here that Turgenev's family stayed for the first few years of the author's life. Although they left the estate in 1822 to travel through Western Europe for a year, and then moved to Moscow in 1824, Turgenev would always be attached to Spasskoe. Turgenev received his education through a series of formal schools and private tutors and was educated in many languages. In 1833, Turgenev's father petitioned Moscow University to waive the age requirement and let Turgenev take his entrance exams early, which he eventually did.

Turgenev was well-read as a child, and became interested in literature very early. His first publication was a poem, "Vecher," which he published in the 1838 issue of *Sovremennik (The Contemporary)*. In the same year, Turgenev left for Germany, where he stayed until 1841. During this time, he made friends with several other Russians and he continued to send his poetry back to Russia for publication. In 1843, when Turgenev was back in Russia, Turgenev's narrative poem, "Parasha," was published, and the author began to be noticed—so much so, in fact, that he never finished his dissertation for his degree, which would have allowed him to teach. The same year, Turgenev was appointed to a post in the Ministry of Internal Affairs, which he left two years later to pursue his writing.

In 1845, Turgenev stepped up his literary efforts, taking part, along with other writers, in the publication of *Sovremennik*, which was under new management. In 1847, he returned to Berlin, although he continued to work on his writing and send selections back to *Sovremennik*. Turgenev returned to Russia in 1850, and the following year, he was imprisoned in St. Petersburg for trying to publish in Moscow an obituary of a fellow writer, Gogol, which had been banned by the St. Petersburg censors. Turgenev's jail time was not long, but he was sent into exile for what turned out to be a two-year term at his Spasskoe estate.

In 1856, Turgenev's first novel, *Rudin*, was published in *Sovremennik*, in two issues. In 1858, he published his short story, "Asia," in *Sovremennik*. The story was one of the first that marked Turgenev as a liberal from the 1840s, and it was this, along with other works, most notably *Fathers and Sons* in 1862, led to a break with *Sovremennik* and with the young radicals.

The novel depicts the problems inherent with the emancipation reforms that freed the Russian serfs. The backlash from the novel's reception discouraged Turgenev from pursuing any major works until 1865, when he began writing his fifth novel, *Dym*, which was published in 1867. Although he would eventually be overshadowed by

Tolstoy and Dostoyevsky, Turgenev was still the first Russian writer who was known worldwide. Turgenev died on August 22, 1883, in his chalet at Bougival.

Plot Summary

Chapters I-III

Fathers and Sons starts with Nikolai Kirsanov eagerly waiting at a posting station—a depot for horse carriages—for his son Arkady, who has just graduated from school. When Arkady arrives, however, his father is surprised to see that he has brought a friend, Bazarov, to stay with him at their farm. Bazarov is an older medical student who serves as Arkady's mentor. He is calm, cool, and dispassionate.

Chapters IV-XI

They reach the farm where Arkady's uncle, Pavel Kirsanov, is happy to see him. Pavel does not care for Bazarov, however, and makes no effort to hide his distaste. Nikolai tries to bring up the subject of his mistress, Fenitchka, delicately, but Arkady charges off to see her, finding out in the process that he has a new baby brother. It does not take long before the two generations start clashing, mainly due to Bazarov's nihilistic ideas, a type of scientific materialism that advocates believing in nothing. These ideas, which Arkady mimics in their conversations, distress the older Kirsanovs, who realize that there is a large generation gap between them and the young men. Nikolai is sad, feeling his son slipping away from him, while Pavel is angry and gets into heated debates with Bazarov. After Nikolai and Pavel decline an invitation to go see their cousin in another provincial town, Bazarov and Arkady accept in their place.

Chapters XII-XV

In the town they meet Matvy Ilyich Kolyazin, Nikolai's cousin, who is an important official. Like Pavel, Kolyazin does not like Bazarov, although he invites both young men to the Governor's Ball. On the road they run into Victor Sitnikov, another one of Bazarov's disciples, who convinces them to pay a visit to Evdoksya Kukshin. Bazarov finds her boring, but still drinks her champagne. Kukshin tells them they should meet Anna Odintsov, a rich young widow, at the Governor's Ball. At the ball Arkady meets Anna and instantly falls in love with her, but she treats him like a friend and asks about Bazarov. After the dance, Arkady lets Bazarov know that Anna is interested in meeting with him and they visit at her hotel. Bazarov is uncharacteristically nervous in her presence. Anna suggests they come see her at Nikolskoe, her country estate, which they do a few days later.

Chapters XVI-XVIII

At Nikolskoe, Anna introduces the two young men to her sister Katya. Bazarov and Arkady stay at the estate for a fortnight, during which time Arkady slowly builds up a friendship with Katya, which starts to blossom into love and override his nihilism.

In the meantime Bazarov is in the throes of a passionate love for Anna, which he finally confesses to her at the end of his stay. However, even though she has been flirting with him, he is dismayed when she spurns his advance. Relations are awkward with all of them until Bazarov and Arkady leave shortly thereafter for Bazarov's parents' house.

Chapters XIX-XXII

Bazarov's parents have not seen him for three years and are expecting a long stay. However, they smother him with affection, which makes him uncomfortable, and he and Arkady stay only three days, much to their dismay. They get on the road to go back to Maryino and pick up Bazarov's scientific instruments but on a whim, Arkady decides to have them go back to Nikolskoe. Anna is not expecting them, and does not seem pleased to see them. They quickly make an excuse, saying that they were not intending on staying and that they have just stopped in on their way to Maryino. Bazarov and Arkady surprise everyone at Maryino, who also were not expecting them back so soon. However, they are glad to see the two young men. Arkady is not long at home, however, before he finds out from his father that he has letters from Katya's mother, who used to write to Arkady's mother. He decides to use the letters as an excuse to visit Nikolskoe again, but this time, he is received warmly by Katya.

Media Adaptations

- *Fathers and Sons* was adapted as an audio book by The Audio Partners Publishing Corporation in 1998 and read by David Horovitch.

- *Ottsy i deti* is the Russian version of *Fathers and Sons*. It was adapted as a film in 1959. It was produced by Lenfilm Studio and distributed by Artkino Pictures.

Chapter XXIII-XXIV

While Arkady is at Nikolskoe, Bazarov busies himself with his scientific experiments at Maryino. He also starts to spend more time with Fenitchka, Nikolai's mistress, under the pretense of offering doctor's remedies to their child. One day, when he is alone with Fenitchka in the garden, he kisses her, and Pavel sees. Shortly thereafter, Pavel challenges him to a secret duel and Bazarov accepts. Bazarov is unharmed, but shoots Pavel in the leg, then bandages the wound for him and stays with him until another doctor comes to relieve him. Bazarov leaves.

Chapters XXV-XXVI

Meanwhile Arkady is starting to express his feelings for Katya, but cannot quite tell her he loves her. Bazarov arrives and stays for a few days. Arkady again tries to express his love for Katya in the garden but is interrupted when they hear Bazarov and Anna walking by, talking about their own failed relationship. They leave and Arkady finally tells Katya he loves her. She returns the sentiment and shortly thereafter, Arkady asks Anna for her sister's hand in marriage. Bazarov leaves.

Chapter XXVII

Bazarov's parents are overjoyed to see him, especially when he tells them that he will be there for six weeks. He is noticeably changed from his experiences. Although he tries to busy himself with his experiments, he finds himself getting more social, talking to peasants, and begins to help his father, another doctor, with his patients. After a patient dies of typhus, Bazarov performs an autopsy, cutting himself in the process. The typhus infection quickly overcomes him, and he dies shortly thereafter. On his deathbed, he sends for Anna, who is with him when he collapses into his final unconscious state before death.

Chapter XXVIII

Six months pass, and in January, both Arkady and his father marry their respective loves. Pavel leaves on the day of the wedding to seek his fortunes abroad. Turgenev addresses the reader, saying that he will give a short synopsis of how everybody is doing in the present. Anna gets married, but not out of love; instead, it is out of the same practical good sense that she has always followed. Arkady, his father, and their respective families live at Maryino, where Arkady is running the now-prosperous farm, while Nikolai helps to institute the upcoming emancipation reforms that will revolutionize Russian society. Pavel spends his time first in Moscow before settling in Dresden, Germany. Finally, Bazarov's parents weep at his grave often, mourning their lost son. Turgenev offers one final thought, saying that love is not hopeless, and that in the end, even Bazarov will have eternal reconciliation and life without end.

Characters

Father Alexey

Father Alexey is a nice priest who comes to visit Bazarov's parents; he wins money from Bazarov at whist, a card game.

Arisha

See Arina Vlasyevna Bazarov

Arkasha

See Arkady Nikolaitch Kirsanov

Arina Vlasyevna Bazarov

Arina Vlasyevna, Bazarov's mother, adores her son and is crushed at his tragic death. When she was younger, Arina was part of the Russian minor nobility, but since she has married, she has turned over all of her affairs to her husband, Vassily. She is still horrified at the upcoming reforms, however, which will divide up the land of the nobility. When Bazarov comes home to visit for the first time in three years, she smothers him with attention, and, as a result, he leaves after three days. When Bazarov comes back for a longer stay, she is more discreet and does not bother him as much. Vassily does not tell Arina about Bazarov's typhus until he is sure his son is infected. After Bazarov's death, his parents visit his grave often, weeping for their son.

Vassily Ivanovitch Bazarov

Vassily Ivanovitch is Bazarov's father and like his wife, Arina, he adores his son. Vassily worked as an army surgeon under Arkady's grandfather, who was a general at the time. In his retirement, Vassily and his wife live in a small country homestead, where Vassily still administers treatment to the peasants for free. When Bazarov comes home, it is the first time he has seen his son in three years, and Bazarov only stays three days, a fact that makes Vassily very sad. When Bazarov comes back, Vassily is overjoyed to hear that Bazarov will be staying for six weeks. Bazarov starts helping his father with his patients, and in the process takes the opportunity to dissect a man who has just died from typhus. When Vassily sees the cut on Bazarov's finger that he gets during the autopsy, he is frightened that his son has caught the disease. A few days later, Bazarov dies, and Vassily's fears come true.

Yevgeny Vassilyev Bazarov

Bazarov, as he is known throughout most of the work, is the friend of Arkady, and he dies at the end of the novel from a typhus infection. Even from the beginning of the novel, Bazarov, a young medical student, is expected by almost everybody to do great things. His unflinching manner and severe conviction to the strict tenets of nihilism—a type of scientific rationalism—have given him many disciples, of which Arkady is one. At the beginning of the book, Bazarov comes to stay with Arkady and his father at Maryino. The visit is full of conflict, as Bazarov's harshly radical ideas clash with Nikolai's brother, Pavel. Bazarov is completely unapologetic, even when Arkady tries to appeal to him. In fact, even though he wounds his friend with his sarcasm, Bazarov does not make amends. He states to all that he does not believe in his own emotions and should not therefore spare others. Bazarov and Arkady leave for a provincial town to meet Arkady's second cousin, who invites them to the Governor's Ball, where Arkady meets Anna Odintsov. The lady has more interest in Bazarov, however, and soon Arkady and Bazarov are staying with her at her country estate.

Although he tries to deny his feelings for Anna, they overcome Bazarov, who professes his love to her on the eve of his departure. She shuns him, however, and he goes instead to stay with his parents. They smother him with their emotion, and he leaves after three days, eventually going back to Maryino. Although he is content at first to busy himself with his scientific experiments, his eyes begin to stray, and at one point, he kisses Fenitchka, Nikolai's mistress. She is not interested in his affections, however, even though she was friendly with him. Pavel sees the kiss and challenges Bazarov to a secret duel. Bazarov accepts and walks away unharmed, although he shoots Pavel in the leg. Bazarov immediately takes care of the wound. He leaves Maryino shortly thereafter, and, after one more brief visit to Nikolskoe to see Anna, he bids his farewell to Arkady and goes to his parents' home. He tries to busy himself with his experiments, but finds himself being more social instead. He also starts to help his father, a retired army surgeon, with the peasant patients who come to him. In the course of performing an autopsy on a typhus victim, he cuts himself and gets typhus himself, which kills him a few days later. On his deathbed, he sends for Anna, who sees him before he dies.

Enyusha

See Yevgeny Vassilyev Bazarov

Fenitchka

See Fedyosa Savishna

The Governor

The Governor throws the ball where Arkady meets Anna Odintsov. He is also the employer of Arkady's second cousin, Matvy Ilyich Kolyazin.

Princess Avdotya Stepanovna H—

Princess H—is the rich and grumpy aunt of Anna and Katya, who comes to live with them after their father dies. Nobody likes her, and nobody remembers her when she is dead.

Katya

See Katerina Sergyevna

Arkady Nikolaitch Kirsanov

Arkady Kirsanov is Bazarov's friend, Nikolai's son, Pavel's nephew and eventually, Katya's husband. When the book begins, Arkady, who is quite impressionable, is under the influence of Bazarov, and is trying desperately to adopt his friend's nihilistic ways. However, it is apparent from very early on that, although Arkady thinks he wants to be a radical, he still enjoys music, nature, and other "irrational" pursuits that distance him from Bazarov and nihilism. In fact, he and Bazarov get in many arguments throughout the novel about their conflicting beliefs. Still, in most cases, Arkady is willing to follow his mentor and does so to many destinations. At the Governor's Ball, it is Arkady who first meets and makes the acquaintance of Anna Odintsov. However, even though he is smitten with her, she only has sisterly love for him, and wants to meet Bazarov. As the two young men stay at Nikolskoe, Anna's country estate, the divide between them grows deeper, as Bazarov spends more time with Anna, and Arkady finds himself increasingly more attracted to Katya.

When Bazarov gets ready to leave Nikolskoe, Arkady is torn. He wants to follow his friend, but he also wants to stay with Katya. He follows his friend, first to Bazarov's parents' house, and then back to Maryino. However, Arkady cannot sit still for long. Finding an excuse to visit Nikolskoe again, he does so, where he finds Katya overjoyed to see him. After staying there for a little longer, Arkady finally gets up his nerve to propose to Katya, which he does after a few attempts. She happily accepts. When Bazarov shows up at Nikolskoe and says his farewell to Arkady, he tells him that he never would have made a good nihilist, and that he should pursue family life. Arkady and Katya are married in a ceremony with his father and Fenitchka. After this, they move into Maryino with the other couple, and Arkady takes over the management of the farm, whipping it into a profitable enterprise once more. At the end of the story, Arkady and Katya also have a son, Nikolai.

Marya Kirsanov

Marya Kirsanov is Nikolai's deceased wife and Arkady's deceased mother. Nikolai names his estate, "Maryino," after her.

Nikolai Petrovich Kirsanov

Nikolai Kirsanov is Arkady's father and Pavel's brother. Nikolai and Pavel's father was a general, so they were both expected to go into military service, which Pavel does. Nikolai, however, breaks his leg on the day he is supposed to leave for service, and is unable to serve. Instead, Nikolai gets his university degree and then works in the civil service position that his father finds for him. However, directly after the mourning period for his parents' deaths, Nikolai quits the civil service position, marries Masha, the daughter of his landlord—something his parents did not approve of—and moves to his country estate to live. When their son Arkady is born, they are joyous but ten years later, Masha dies. Nikolai spends more time with his son, even going to stay three years in town to be by his son while he is attending college, getting to know his son's friends.

For his son's last year, however, he does not stay, so he is surprised by the arrival of Bazarov at Maryino when Arkady graduates and comes home. Nikolai is gracious to Bazarov, but is also distressed at the young man's nihilistic views. Nikolai feels the generation gap widening between him and his son. Meanwhile, he has had a child with Fenitchka, the young daughter of his old housekeeper. Although he has held off from marrying her out of respect for his brother, Pavel, whom he does not think believes in marriage. Pavel eventually encourages him to marry. Nikolai gets married to Fenitchka in the same ceremony where Arkady marries Katya. This double wedding, and Arkady's choice to start running his father's farm, helps to close the generation gap.

Pavel Petrovich Kirsanov

Pavel Kirsanov is Nikolai's brother, Arkady's uncle, and Bazarov's opponent; when he challenges

Bazarov to a duel, the younger man wounds him, then tends to the wound. When he was younger, Pavel had a promising military career, which he ruined when he resigned his commission to chase after a married woman, Princess R—. Although the two do have an affair, it is torturous for both and she eventually ends it, after he has chased her through many countries, and they have one final meeting. Pavel tries to resume his normal life but he is a broken man. The only remnant of his disciplined officer days are the smart clothes and nail polish that he wears, even when lounging casually around Maryino, Nikolai's home, where he lives. Pavel occasionally bails Nikolai out when he has money problems.

When Pavel first sees Bazarov, he does not like him, an animosity that grows as Bazarov gives his nihilistic beliefs. They get in many arguments and on Bazarov's second visit, they appear to be at peace. When Pavel catches Bazarov kissing his brother's mistress, however, he challenges Bazarov to a secret duel with pistols. Bazarov accepts and walks away unhurt. Pavel, however, gets shot in the leg. Through the experience of getting shot, getting tended by Bazarov, and recuperating in Maryino, Pavel is able to finally put his past behind and get on with his life. After the dual wedding of his brother and nephew, Pavel goes to Moscow, then finally settles in Germany, where he renews his old social habits for which he was famous as an officer.

Ilya Kolyazin

See Matvy Ilyich Kolyazin

Matvy Ilyich Kolyazin

Matvy Ilyich Kolyazin is Arkady's second cousin, a high-ranking official and the one who invites Arkady and Bazarov to the Governor's Ball where Arkady meets Anna Odintsov. Kolyazin is the cousin of Nikolai and Pavel, and originally extends the visitation invitation to them, but they turn it down. Arkady and Bazarov go in their place.

Madame Evdoksya Kukshin

Madame Kukshin is a friend of Victor Sitnikov, who tells Arkady and Bazarov they should seek out Anna Odintsov. Arkady and Bazarov only agree to meet Kukshin with the promise by Sitnikov of free alcohol. Kukshin tries to impress Arkady and Bazarov with her advanced ways of thinking. She is an independent woman who runs her own affairs now that she is separated from her husband. At the end of the novel, she goes to Heidelberg, Germany to study architecture.

Sergay Nikolaevitch Loktev

Sergay Loktev is Anna Odintsov's father, who loses much of the family fortune playing cards, prompting Anna to marry for money after his death.

Masha

See Marya Kirsanov

Mitya

Mitya is the child of Nikolai and Fenitchka. The child is born out of wedlock, but the couple marries by the end of the story.

Nellie

See Princess R—

Avdotya Nikitishna

See Madame Evdoksya Kukshin

Fedyosa Nikolaevna

See Fedyosa Savishna

Madame Anna Sergyevna Odintsov

Madame Anna Odintsov is the love interest of both Arkady and Bazarov, and ends up shunning both. Anna acts like a mother to her sister Katya, ever since their father's death. After his death, Anna marries a wealthy man to better her financial position and she and Katya retire to Nikolskoe where they live in isolation. Anna's neighbors do not like her because of the rumors that surround her and her father's scandalous gambling debts. Shortly after they move into Nikolskoe, their aunt Princess H—, a surly woman whom nobody likes, moves into Nikolskoe. Anna takes it all in stride and sticks to her principles of keeping everything orderly, including people.

Anna first meets Arkady at the Governor's Ball, where he talks to her at length, but she shows only sisterly interest in him. She does, however, ask to meet Bazarov, and does shortly thereafter when Arkady and Bazarov come to her hotel room. While she is calm, Bazarov is struck by love and behaves irrationally for perhaps the first time in his life. She invites them to come see her at Nikolskoe, her country estate, and they do so a few days later. Although Anna, Katya, Arkady, and Bazarov start out in each other's company, over the next fortnight they split into two couples—Anna and Bazarov; Katya and Arkady. When she is alone with Bazarov, Anna flirts with him, but then rejects his advances when he professes his love for her. She is scared of his passion and wishes to live her orderly life. After she approves of Katya's marriage to Arkady, Anna eventually remarries also, this time to a politically powerful lawyer—as before, it is out of opportunity, not love. She responds to Bazarov's deathbed summons, seeing him one last time before he dies.

Piotr

Piotr is one of the few freed serfs that Nikolai keeps employed at Maryino. Piotr also serves as the witness at the duel between Bazarov and Pavel.

Porfiry Platonitch

Porfiry Platonitch is the card-playing neighbor of Anna Odintsov's, and one of few regular visitors to Nikolskoe.

Princess R—

Princess R— is the woman with whom Pavel Kirsanov falls in love. Both are tormented by the relationship, which she finally ends by running away from Pavel. On her deathbed, she sends Pavel back his ring.

Fedosya Savishna

Fedosya Savishna, also known as Fenitchka, is Nikolai's mistress. Fenitchka is the daughter of Nikolai's housekeeper, who comes to live with Nikolai while Arkady is at school. Although she is shy around Nikolai at first, at one point, he helps to heal her eye from a spark that has flown into it. After this, she starts to warm up to him. When her mother dies from cholera, Nikolai begins to have his affair with her, which results in the birth of Mitya. When Arkaday comes home from school, he has heard about Fenitchka, but has not met her. Although Fenitchka is shy around him, and indeed around everyone, she gradually starts to open up. Bazarov introduces himself as a doctor, after which she comes to see him for various questions about Mitya. At one point, in the garden, Bazarov oversteps his bounds and kisses her. Although they had been having playful conversation, she did not want this, and lets him know. Pavel witnesses the incident, and later confronts her on it, but it is only to make sure that she is truly in love with Nikolai. Pavel encourages Nikolai and Fenitchka to get married, which they do with Arkady and Katya. At the end of the book, Fenitchka loves nothing more than conversing with her daughter-in-law, Katya.

Katerina Sergyevna

Katerina Sergyevna, also known as Katya, is the sister of Anna Odintsov, and marries Arkady Kirsanov. When Anna first introduces Katya to Arkady and Bazarov, neither one is interested in her. They are both in love with Anna. Bazarov views her as a pupil, who could be molded into whatever they want. However, after a while, Arkady's love for Anna fades, and, through a slow but steady friendship at Nikolskoe, Arkady falls in love with Katya, denouncing many of his nihilistic beliefs in the process. When he proposes to her, it takes him a few tries to get the words out, but she gives him an immediate "yes." Katy and Arkady are married in the same ceremony as Fenitchka and Nikolai.

Victor Sitnikov

Victor Sitnikov is the overeager disciple of Bazarov, who introduces Arkady and Bazarov to Evdoksya Kukshin. Sitnikov wants to be a true nihilist, but shows too much emotion for Bazarov's taste. For their part, both Arkady and Bazarov treat Sitnikov badly, ignoring him, making sarcastic remarks, and deliberately taking a carriage other than his.

Vasya

See Vassily Ivanovitch Bazarov

Themes

The Generation Gap

The very title of the novel indicates one of the major themes. The gap between the older and younger generation is very pronounced, especially between fathers and their sons. Nikolai Kirsanov notes to his brother, Pavel, how they are "behind the times" and that the younger generation has surpassed them. He is wistful, however, at the implications of this gap: "I did so hope, precisely now, to get on to such close, intimate terms with Arkady, and it turns out I'm left behind, and he has gone forward, and we can't understand one another."

Bazarov's father makes a similar observation, when he gets into a discussion about new versus old ideas: "Of course, gentlemen, you know best; how could we keep pace with you? You are here to take our places." This gap seems to grow between them as they talk, and the old man tries to fit in by telling a funny story: "The old man was alone in his laughter; Arkady forced a smile on his face. Bazarov simply stretched. The conversation went on in this way for about an hour." When Bazarov's father complains about this fact to his wife, she tells him that there is "no help for it, Vasya! A son is a separate piece cut off."

Although Bazarov's early death prevents him

and his father from closing their generation gap, the case is different for Arkady and Nikolai: "A week before in the small parish church two weddings had taken place quietly.... Arkady and Katya's, and Nikolai Petrovitch and Fenitchka's." The double wedding leads to Arkady and Katya staying at Maryino, where Arkady eventually pitches in and runs his father's estate for him. As Turgenev's narrator says, "their fortunes are beginning to mend."

Poverty

Poverty is a very real issue in the story, even for formerly wealthy landowners like Nikolai. In the beginning, when Nikolai's farm, Maryino, is described, the peasant's portion is depicted as follows: "the peasants they met were all in tatters and on the sorriest little nags; the willows, with their trunks stripped of bark, and broken branches, stood like ragged beggars along the roadside." The peasants are not the only ones who feel the pinch. Nikolai often "sighed, and was gloomy; he felt that the thing could not go on without money, and his money was almost spent." For these reasons, Nikolai's farm is infamous; "the peasants had nicknamed it, Poverty Farm."

Bazarov's parents are even poorer. When Arkady first arrives at the residence, the reader sees that "his whole house consisted of six tiny rooms." And, as Vassily Ivanovitch notes: "I warned you, my dear Arkady Nikolaitch … that we live, so to say, bivouacking." This military term, from Vassily's time in the military service, denotes a rougher lifestyle akin to camping in the rough.

Nihilism

In the story, Turgenev sets up a conflict between the older generation of fathers who believe in art and other irrational activities, and the nihilists —scientific materialists like Bazarov who accept nothing. Bazarov is very critical of anything that does not serve a purpose, especially art. "A good chemist is twenty times as useful as any poet," Bazarov tells them.

For their part, the older generation of Kirsanov men does not agree. Says Pavel to Bazarov, "If we listen to you, we shall find ourselves outside humanity, outside its laws." Furthermore, Nikolai tells Bazarov that he does more than "deny everything … you destroy everything…. But one must construct too, you know." For Bazarov and other nihilists, leveling society and starting with a clean slate is the only way to get rid of "our leading men, so-called advanced people and reformers," who "are no good." Being a liberal himself, Nikolai understands his son's desire for reform, but cannot understand the total exclusion of the arts: "But to renounce poetry?… to have no feeling for art, for nature?"

As for Arkady, Bazarov's disciple, he finds it tough to maintain his nihilistic attitude as the novel goes on: "In his heart he was highly delighted with his friend's suggestion, but he thought it a duty to conceal his feeling. He was not a nihilist for nothing!" By the end of the novel, Arkady has totally forsaken his nihilistic beliefs for marriage, music, and nature, three ideas that nihilism does not allow. Bazarov also experiences a change by the end of the novel. After he is slighted by Anna following his unprecedented profession of love, he tells her, "Before you is a poor mortal, who has come to his senses long ago, and hopes other people, too, have forgotten his follies."

Bazarov has started to realize the error of his ways. While he is staying with his parents, they notice it too. "A strange weariness began to show itself in all his movements; even his walk, firm, bold and strenuous, was changed. He gave up walking in solitude, and began to seek society." And when he is dying from typhus, he encourages his parents "to make the most of your religious belief; now's the time to put it to the test." Although, it is telling that when Bazarov has the chance to try to save his soul with his parents' religion, he declines. Even though he has changed, allowed himself to love, and admitted the folly of some of his ways, he is not ready to embrace religion even on his deathbed.

Topics for Further Study

- Research the specific beliefs of both the young radicals from the 1860s and the older liberals from the 1840s in Russia. Create a picture, story, or some other sort of artistic effort in which half of the item represents the ideas of the radicals and half represents the liberals. Somewhere on this item, indicate the qualities you are trying to demonstrate for each half.

- Read Albert Camus's *The Stranger* and compare Camus's existentialist narrator to Bazarov. What are the similarities and differences between nihilism and existentialism?

- Research the current state of affairs in Russia, noting any particular reform efforts that are going on. How do these differ from reforms that were happening in the mid-1800s?

- Research Russian art from the mid-1800s until the end of the nineteenth century and discuss whether it did or did not take a revolutionary approach, like much literature did. In either case, find one painting that you like and write a report giving your interpretation of what the painting means, as well as any historical significance it may have.

- Research the complex history surrounding the emancipation of the serfs in Russia in the 1860s and their gradual establishment as landowners. Write a journal entry from the perspective of either a recently freed serf or a former member of the landed aristocracy, describing your views on the emancipation reforms. Incorporate your research into your entry where necessary.

- Suppose Bazarov had not died from typhus at the end of the book and an extra chapter had been added on to talk about what happened to him in the end. Based on the transformation he undergoes in the novel, how do you predict he would have spent the rest of his life? Write a short plot summary detailing what would take place in this extra chapter.

Love

The idea of romantic love permeates the novel and is most apparent with Arkady and Bazarov, who experience two different types of love. Arkady experiences a love that is based on friendship. Before he even meets his true love, Katya, he is smitten by Madame Anna Odintsov. Unfortunately, the older woman looks at him "as married sisters look at very young brothers." With Katya, however, the situation is different, even from the start. He "encouraged her to express the impressions made on her by music, reading novels, verses, and other such trifles, without noticing or realizing that these trifles were what interested him too." From this tentative friendship, their love starts to blossom, and Arkady's love for Katya starts to replace his love for Madame Odintsov: "He began to imagine Anna Sergyevna to himself, then other features gradually eclipsed the lovely young image of the young widow."

The night before Arkady plans on leaving Nikolskoe with Bazarov, he is distraught: "I'm sorry to lose Katya too!" Arkady whispered to his pillow, on which a tear had already fallen." Eventually Arkady becomes so attached to Katya that he is ecstatic when he arrives unannounced and sees her first: "His meeting with her struck him as a particularly happy omen; he was delighted to see her, as though she were of his own kindred." Finally, Arkady owns up to his feelings, and eventually lets her know that "My eyes have been opened lately, thanks to one feeling." The feeling is love, but in Arkady's case, it is a love that builds slowly from friendship.

For Bazarov, on the other hand, the love is more passionate, forceful. Bazarov shows the signs of an irrational love at his first meeting with Anna. While she is sitting calmly, "leaning back in her easy-chair," and "He, contrary to his habit, was talking a good deal, and obviously trying to interest her—again a surprise for Arkady." As Bazarov stays at Nikolskoe, he begins to exhibit "signs of an unrest, unprecedented in him … and could not sit still in one place, just as though he were possessed by some secret longing."

For her part, Anna gives Bazarov her terms for love: "My idea is everything or nothing. A life for a life. Take mine, give up thine, and that without regret or turning back. Or else better have nothing." Bazarov takes these conversations as a sign that Anna loves him and on the eve of his departure, lets her know that "I love you like a fool, like a madman … There, you've forced it out of me." However, Anna's intentions are not amorous, so her words are crushing to the passionate lover who has let his emotions overtake him for the first time: "You have misunderstood me."

Setting

The setting in *Fathers and Sons* is crucial to the effect of the novel. The various provincial settings—Maryino, Nikolskoe, Vassily Ivanovitch's unnamed homestead—are seen as backward and uneducated when compared with the cities, which are vibrant with new ideas and scholarship. As Bazarov notes to Arkady at one point, if they were to look at their fathers' country existence from a certain perspective, it could be seen as enjoyable, having a routine to keep busy: "When one gets a side view from a distance of the dead-alive life our 'fathers' lead here, one thinks, What could be better?" However, for Bazarov, this life could only ever be "dead-alive," unlike Arkady. On a different occasion, Arkady, who likes the nature one finds in the country, challenges Bazarov: "And is nature foolery?" Arkady hopes to stump Bazarov, but the nihilist is not disturbed and as always, has an answer: "Nature, too, is foolery in the sense you understand it. Nature's not a temple, but a workshop, and man's the workman in it." For Bazarov, nature is something to be dissected as he does with the frogs, or otherwise observed from a scientific viewpoint. Arkady cannot do this, however, and he eventually comes to prefer the country, moving into Maryino with his new wife and his father's family, where Arkady becomes "zealous in the management of the estate" and turns it into a prosperous affair.

Irony

A situation is ironic when its outcome is contrary to what the character and reader expects. In Turgenev's novel this happens many times. For example, Vassily Ivanovitch describes the bitter irony of the generation gap when talking to his son and Arkady about a philosopher of whom they are enamored: "you bow down to him, but in another twenty years it will be his turn to be laughed at." Bazarov and Arkady feel strong and invincible in their youth, as if their ideas are the only ones and they will never be refuted. However, when Arkady's son grows up, Arkady will no doubt realize, as Nikolai does, that aging and the decline of one's ideas is "a bitter pill" and that every new generation is ready to tell the old to "swallow your pill."

Other ironic situations are introduced in the character of Bazarov, whom the reader is led to believe from the beginning cannot be swayed to love. Bazarov is against love because there is no control over it, and it overpowers the senses that he holds dear and by which he rules his life. It is ironic, therefore, that Bazarov is stricken blind with love for Anna, and admits to her, "I love you like a fool, like a madman." It is also ironic that Bazarov, the character who is depicted in an almost god-like, invincible light, is refuted in his advance, from Anna, who seems on the verge of giving her heart to

Bazarov.

The cruelest irony of the novel, however, is the death of Bazarov. The young nihilist who appreciates the hard sciences more than anything else goes to the village, "where they brought that peasant with typhus fever." Although there is a doctor there who is going to dissect the body, Bazarov, always eager for scientific knowledge, offers to do it. Unfortunately, in the process, he makes a careless mistake and cuts himself, contracting the infection that soon kills him. It is tragically ironic that Bazarov's quest for knowledge is the thing that kills him in the end.

Point of View

The novel is told by a third person omniscient, or all-knowing, narrator who has the power to go within any character's mind and display their thoughts. For example, when Bazarov and Pavel get in their first argument over their beliefs, Nikolai thinks to himself, "You are certainly a nihilist, I see that," although what he says aloud is "Still, you will allow me to apply to you on occasion." This is the style for most of the novel. However, there is a notable exception in the narration: at times, the narrator speaks directly to the reader, as when the narrator introduces Nikolai: "We will introduce him to the reader while he sits, his feet tucked under him, gazing thoughtfully round." This style is also used at the end of the novel: "But perhaps some one of our readers would care to know what each of the characters we have introduced is doing in the present." By book-ending the story with these two references that draw attention to the narrator, readers are reminded that they are reading a work of art and are encouraged to focus on the realities of the social situation the book describes—instead of just getting caught up in the story.

Historical Context

Fathers and Sons is tied to Russia's history, particularly to the period of social unrest and reform that began to come to a head with the rule of Alexander II. Following the Crimean War, during which Alexander came to power in 1855, Russian society—and Alexander himself—was made painfully aware of Russia's backward place in the world. These were old concerns that were reawakened with the loss of about 250,000 men and some of Russia's land.

This war was not received well in society and as a result, Alexander, who had been taught by an artistic, romantic tutor, and who was sympathetic to liberal concerns, sought reform. Pitting himself against the landowners who owned serfs, Alexander began to talk about abolishing serfdom. Says Victor Ripp, in his *Turgenev's Russia: From "Notes of a Hunter" to "Fathers and Sons"*: "The Emancipation Act was signed by Alexander II on February 19, 1861, a little less than five years after he had openly declared his support for the abolition of serfdom." In the time between Alexander's announcement of the abolishment and the actual abolishment, Russia underwent some drastic changes as the nation prepared itself for reform.

In this time of uneasiness, Turgenev chose to set his book. As Ripp notes, "it is the spring of 1859, and the emancipation of the serfs, with all its

uncertain consequences, is only two years ahead."
Even two years before this historic event the effects
could be seen in many locations. Nikolai Petrovitch,
a more liberal landowner, has already freed his serfs
before he is required to, although he is wary about
giving his former slaves any control in any major
business affairs. Says Nikolai: "I decided not to
keep about me any freed serfs, who have been
house servants, or, at least, not to intrust them with
duties of any responsibility."

Not everybody was as enlightened as Nikolai,
however. Some, especially the older Russian
nobility with much land to lose, decried the reforms,
like Bazarov's mother. She used to be a member of
the landed gentry, but turned her land over to the
care of her husband, a poor, retired army surgeon.
She "used to groan, wave her handkerchief, and
raise her eyebrows higher and higher with horror
when her old husband began to discuss the
impending government reforms."

However, those who observed the decline of
Russia, as Arkady does in the novel, realized that
reform was sorely needed: "this is not a rich
country; it does not impress one by plenty or
industry; it can't, it can't go on like this, reforms are
absolutely necessary." Of course, as Arkady notes
shortly thereafter, "how is one to carry them out,
how is one to begin?" There seemed to be no clear
answer to that, since Russia was mired in
corruption, which, even though it started at higher
levels, worked its way down. As the narrator notes
of the young governor's official sent to a provincial

town, he "was a young man, and at once a progressive and a despot, as often happens with Russians." This young man is both a sympathetic liberal and a tyrant when he is given the power to abuse. The same was true about the behavior of the lower classes. When given any power at all, they abused it, as Nikolai's farm manager does: "The overseer suddenly turned lazy, and began to grow fat, as every Russian grows fat when he gets a snug berth." Likewise, once Nikolai puts the peasants on a rent system and does not enforce it, he has problems. "The peasants who had been put on the rent system did not bring their money at the time due, and stole the forest-timber."

Even when the serfs were about to be emancipated in 1861, the actual Emancipation Act caused much confusion. As Ripp notes, "In its efforts to please all factions, the Editing Committee produced an immensely complicated document." This general feeling of failure on the part of the Emancipation Act is expressed in the novel through the character of Nikolai, who is entrusted to carry out the upcoming reforms at the end of the novel. He drives around his district, giving long speeches that say the same thing over and over again, but as Turgenev's narrator notes, "to tell the truth, he does not give complete satisfaction either to the refined gentry … nor to the uncultivated gentry…. He is too soft-hearted for both sets." Neither the landed class nor the lower classes wanted a hesitant legislation, but unfortunately, in its attempts to please everyone, the Emancipation Act pleased almost no one and eventually led to more unrest. As Ripp notes,

Turgenev is aware of all of this as he writes the book in 1862, a year after the act has been implemented: "Turgenev wrote *Fathers and Sons*, his greatest novel, while directly under the influence of the crisis caused by the Emancipation Act."

Compare & Contrast

- **1860s:** Under the leadership of Alexander II Russia embarks on a number of social reforms, including abolishing serfdom and improving communications, such as establishing more railroad lines.

  Today: Russia remains a poor and unstable country after the fall of the Soviet Union at the end of the twentieth century. In the wake of the brutal dictatorial regime that ruled "communist" Russia and other Soviet countries for much of the twentieth century, the plight of many Russians has worsened.

- **1860s:** Like those in other countries, many of Russia's youth adhere to a scientific materialism philosophy, questioning everything with a strict rationalism and not letting any "irrational" behavior overcome them.

  Today: In many civilized countries

there is a resurgence in art, nature, and other humanistic pursuits, due in large part to humanity's increasing dependence upon technology.

- **1860s:** Although modern medicine is improving with the such developments as vaccines, the "germ theory" of disease, and improved sanitation in hospitals, doctors are largely powerless. When cholera sweeps across Europe and Russia, many are killed.

Today: In most modernized countries, cholera and typhus, which are usually prevalent in poor, unsanitary areas, have been wiped out. Epidemic typhus persists in countries that experience famine, crowded living conditions, and other areas where sanitation is an issue. Cholera, on the other hand, has been largely dormant, and has not seen a major outbreak for more than a decade.

Critical Overview

In 1862, when Turgenev first gave the manuscript for *Fathers and Sons* to his editor Mikhail Nikiforovich Katkov, the *Russkii vestnik (Russian Herald)* editor was concerned about the potential backlash over the novel.

Katkov had reason to be concerned. As Edward Garnett notes in his *Turgenev*, "the stormy controversy that the novel immediately provoked was so bitter, deep, and lasting that the episode forms one of the most interesting chapters in literary history." The controversy originated in the interpretation of the novel by the two main political forces in Russia at the time—the older liberals, or reactionaries, from the 1840s who were of Turgenev's generation, and the younger radicals— whom Turgenev called "nihilists" in the novel—of the current, 1860s generation. It was with this second group that Turgenev had found favor with through the publication of some of his earlier works in *Sovremennik (Contemporary)*. However, the same critics who had praised Turgenev's earlier works now offered harsh criticism for *Fathers and Sons* as they had for Turgenev's previous novel, *Nakanune*. One of the most vocal critics from *The Contemporary* was M. A. Antonovich, who remarked that Bazarov "is not a man, but some horrible being, simply a devil or, to express oneself more poetically, a foul fiend."

Another radical critic, A. I. Gertsen, notes that in the book, "gloomy, concentrated energy has spoken in this *unfriendly* attitude of the young generation to its mentors." The overwhelming majority of criticisms, both good and bad, concerned the character Bazarov. D. I. Pisarev, another of the younger radicals, was the only critic from his political party who did not describe Bazarov as a "vicious caricature" of the radicals, as Leonard Schapiro notes in *Turgenev: His Life and Times*. Instead, Pisarev writes to both radicals and liberals: "You may be indignant about people like Bazarov to your heart's content, but it is most essential to acknowledge their sincerity."

The book was also disliked by the liberals, many of whom blamed Turgenev's book for the violence exhibited by young radicals. Turgenev himself recounts what is now a famous anecdote from his life, when he returned to Petersburg in 1862 on the same day that young radicals—calling themselves "nihilists"—were setting fire to buildings: "the first exclamation to fall from the lips of the first acquaintance I encountered … was: 'Look what *your* nihilists are doing! Burning Petersburg!'"

The major problem in the book's reception was the fact that both radicals and liberals thought that the book was aimed against them, especially in the portrayal of Bazarov. This problem was underscored by Turgenev's own conflicting views on the character. Although he stated in a March 30 letter to Fyodor Dostoyevsky that "during all the time of writing I have felt an involuntary attraction for him," he stated in a different letter on April 18 to A. A. Fet: "Did I wish to curse Bazarov, or extol him? *I don't know that myself*, for I don't know if I love or hate him!"

In 1881, William Ralston Shedden-Ralston, one of Turgenev's English friends, publicized the author's upcoming visit by noting that Turgenev was "the wielder of a style unrivalled for delicacy and seldom equalled in force," and that "it will be easy to see that in his own field he stands alone." George Moore notes of Bazarov that "he is a real creation, not a modernisation of some Shakespearean or classical conception, but an absolutely new and absolutely distinct addition made to our knowledge of life." The famous American-born, English writer and critic, Henry James, notes the novel's "poignant interest," that is created by the "young world" smiting "the old world which has brought it forth with a mother's tears and a mother's hopes."

During the twentieth century, reviews were largely positive, as reviewers focused on Turgenev's artistic techniques and prophetic powers. Peter Henry notes that "it is a brilliant stroke of irony on Turgenev's part that Bazarov and Pavel Petrovich, so sharply contrasted in every way, are endowed with an essential identity as unsuccessful lovers." In his *Turgenev: The Man, His Art and His Age*, Avrahm Yarmolinsky says that "throughout, his craftsmanship is at its best. Even the minor characters are deftly sketched in." And Isaiah Berlin notes that today, "the Bazarovs have won," since the world is ruled by technology and empirical science.

Sources

Antonovich, M. A., "Asmodey nashego vremeni (An Asmodeus of our Time)," in *Fathers and Children*, edited by Patrick Waddington, Everyman, p. 253, originally published in *Sovremennik (The Contemporary)*, No. 3, 1862.

Berlin, Isaiah, Lecture on *Fathers and Children*, in *Fathers and Children*, edited by Patrick Waddington, Everyman, p. 272, originally published in *"Fathers and Children": the Romanes Lecture, delivered in the Sheldonian Theatre, 12 November 1970*, Oxford University Press, 1972, pp. 55-56.

Engel, Barbara Alpern, Excerpt, in *Fathers and Children*, edited by Patrick Waddington, Everyman, p. 273, originally published in *Mothers and Daughters: Women of the Intelligentsia in Nineteenth-Century Russia*, Cambridge University Press, 1983, p. 63.

Garnett, Edward, *Turgenev*, Kennikat Press, 1966, p. 110.

Gertsen, A. I., "Yeshchéraz Bazarov (Bazarov Again)," in *Fathers and Children*, edited by Patrick Waddington, Everyman, p. 257, originally published in *Polyarnaya zvezda (The Pole Star)*, 1869.

Henry, Peter, "I. S. Turgenev: *Fathers and Sons*," in *Fathers and Children*, edited by Patrick

Waddington, Everyman, p. 277-78, originally published in *The Monster in the Mirror: Studies in Nineteenth-Century Realism*, edited by D. A. Williams, Oxford University Press, 1978, pp. 55-56.

James, Henry, "Ivan Turgéenieff," in *Fathers and Children*, edited by Patrick Waddington, Everyman, p. 267, originally published in *North American Review*, Vol. CXVIII, April 1874, pp. 326-56.

Moore, George, "Turgueneff," in *Fathers and Children*, edited by Patrick Waddington, Everyman, p. 265-66, originally published in *Fortnightly Review*, n.s., Vol. XLIII, February 1, 1888, pp. 244-46.

Pisarev, D. I., "Bazarov," in *Fathers and Children*, edited by Patrick Waddington, Everyman, p. 255, originally published in *Russkoye slovo (The Russian Word)*, No. 3, 1862.

Ripp, Victor, *Turgenev's Russia: From "Notes of a Hunter" to "Fathers and Sons,"* Cornell University Press, 1980, pp. 187, 190-91.

Schapiro, Leonard, *Turgenev: His Life and Times*, Random House, 1978, p. 185.

Shedden-Ralston, William Ralston, "Ivan Turguenief," in *Fathers and Children*, edited by Patrick Waddington, Everyman, p. 265, originally published in *Saturday Review*, October 22, 1881, p. 509.

Turgenev, Ivan, *Fathers and Sons*, Barnes & Noble Classics, 2000.

⸺, "Letter to A. A. Fet, Paris, 16

April 1862," in *Fathers and Children*, edited by Patrick Waddington, Everyman, p. 246, originally published in *Literaturnyye i zhiteyskiye vospominaniya* (Memories of Life and Literature), 1869, and subsequently translated into English and published in *I. S. Turgenev, Complete Works and Letters in 28 vols*, Moscow and Leningrad: Nauka, 1960–1968 (Letters), Vol. IV, p. 371.

——————————————, "Letter to F. M. Dostoyevsky, Paris, 30 March 1862," in *Fathers and Children*, edited by Patrick Waddington, Everyman, p. 245, originally published in *Literaturnyye i zhiteyskiye vospominaniya* (Memories of Life and Literature), 1869, and subsequently translated into English and published in *I. S. Turgenev, Complete Works and Letters in 28 vols*, Moscow and Leningrad: Nauka, 1960–1968 (Letters), Vol. IV, pp. 358-59.

——————————————, "On *Fathers and Children*," in *Fathers and Children*, edited by Patrick Waddington, Everyman, p. 251, originally published in *Literaturnyye i zhiteyskiye vospominaniya* (Memories of Life and Literature), 1869, and subsequently translated into English and published in *I. S. Turgenev, Complete Works and Letters in 28 vols*, Moscow and Leningrad: Nauka, 1960–1968 (Works), Vol. XIV, pp. 97-99, 103-05.

Yarmolinsky, Avrahm, *Turgenev: The Man, His Art and His Age*, Collier Books, 1959, p. 199.

Further Reading

Costlow, Jane Tussey, *Worlds within Worlds: The Novels of Ivan Turgenev*, Princeton University Press, 1990.

> Turgenev's books are well known for the accurate portrayal of life within his time. The author discusses this aspect of his writing combined with his exquisite style for words.

Freeborn, Richard, *The Russian Revolutionary Novel: Turgenev to Pasternak*, Cambridge University Press, 1985.

> Turgenev and Pasternak are just two of the Russian writers who faced persecution for their revolutionary works. One of the richest periods in Russian literature spans from the novels of Turgenev's time in the middle of the nineteenth century to those of Pasternak in the middle of the twentieth century.

Hayek, F. A., *The Road to Serfdom*, University of Chicago Press, 1994.

> Ahead of its time when first published in 1947, this book discusses the dangers to a society when the government gains increasing economic control. Hayek

focuses mainly on the tyrannies of his time in Germany, Italy, and Soviet Russia, which were based on National Socialism. In this classic text, Hayek foresaw the failure of socialism.

Kolchin, Peter, *Unfree Labor: American Slavery and Russian Serfdom*, Belknap Press, 1990.

Kolchin's acclaimed comparative history study examines the institutions of slavery and serfdom in America and Russia respectively, including the emancipation efforts.

Lowe, David A., *Critical Essays on Ivan Turgenev*, Macmillan Library Reference, 1988.

This book contains reprinted criticism—reviews and essays—that was originally published in the early to late twentieth century. The criticism was originally published in English, German, and Russian.

Roosevelt, Priscilla, *Life on the Russian Country Estate: A Social and Cultural History*, Yale University Press, 1997.

The author gives a historical account of the rural, Russian aristocratic landowner class, which survived the emancipation of the serfs and was visible even at the end of the century. The book features many images and illustrations of a cultural world that has since vanished.

Waddington, Patrick, *Ivan Turgenev and Britain*, Berg Publishers Incorporated, 1995.

This book discusses the influence that Britain had on Ivan Turgenev. The author visited England often and associated with many of the English literary class, including Tennyson and George Eliot. The book also reprints some previously unpublished articles and features an extensive bibliography.

CPSIA information can be obtained
at www.ICGtesting.com
Printed in the USA
BVHW040643200821
614843BV00023B/629